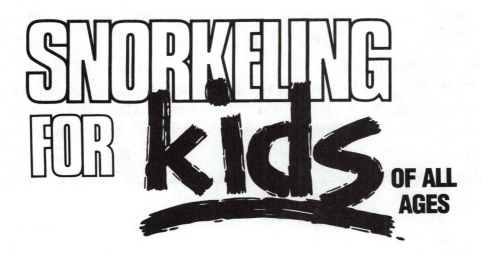

Snorkeling for Kids
Second Edition

National Association of Underwater Instructors
PO Box 14650 Montclair, California 91763 USA

Written by Judith Jennet
Illustrations by Nadine Nakanishi
Environmental Content provided by Hillary Viders, PhD

The NAUI Mission

To promote and encourage through purposeful activity the education and training of the general public in the safety and techniques of participating in underwater activities, and to educate people to preserve and protect the quality of the underwater environment.

Text and illustrations Copyright 1992 by NAUI
ISBN 0-916974-50-2
Published by the National Association of Underwater Instructors
PO Box 14650, Montclair, CA 91763 • (714) 621-5801

Printed in the United States of America
10 9 8 7 6 5 4 3 2 1

TABLE OF CONTENTS

This book can be the best snorkeling buddy you'll ever have. Here an experienced snorkeling instructor uses the most up-to-date know-how to answer your questions about snorkeling as simply as possible. Remember though, no book can replace personal contact with a qualified and caring NAUI scuba diving or snorkeling instructor.

the SNORKELER'S Environment

How We Care for Mother Earth

THE SNORKELER'S ENVIRONMENT

HOW WE CAN CARE FOR MOTHER EARTH

Once you learn to snorkel, you will discover a whole new world — the world underwater. You can be an **explorer** and find **adventure** in the ocean, a river, a lake, or even your swimming pool. But of all the places, the most exciting and most beautiful is the ocean.

The ocean is like a huge city, filled with **beautiful** and **wondrous creatures**. It is one of the most important places on our planet. The ocean is important because it provides a home and food for billions of fish, plants, and animals.

There are children in many countries of the world that would go hungry if not for the food they get from the ocean. Scientists also explore the ocean to discover new life forms, to learn about climate and to find new medicines to keep us healthy.

The creatures in the underwater environment come in all sizes and shapes. In order to survive they live in a system that is organized and carefully balanced. This balanced system is called a **marine ecosystem**. As snorkelers, we must be very careful not to disturb the balance in a marine ecosystem.

Coral reefs are the most **fragile** of all marine ecosystems. Coral is fragile because it can only live in water that is warm, clear, and very salty. Coral also needs a lot of sunlight, so it can make food by a process called "photosynthesis." Corals are a combination of both tiny animals and plants. Corals can be hard or soft. Hard coral is the kind that builds a coral reef, by adding outer layers of limestone skeletons over many years. There are many types of hard coral that you may see while snorkeling the ocean. Some of them have funny names like brain coral, elkhorn coral and lettuce leaf coral. Corals build reefs very slowly. It may take thousands of years to grow just a few feet tall!

THE FOOD CHAIN OF A CORAL REEF

In the coral reef, the different creatures depend on a **food chain** which must not be broken. A food chain means that every creature has plants or animals in the ocean which it can eat. Every day each creature in the ocean must struggle to find its food, while trying not to become another creature's dinner! It is important that we do not break this food chain by taking things out of the ocean or putting into the ocean anything that doesn't belong there.

Most of the creatures you will see while snorkeling are **shy** and **gentle**, and will not harm you. But many of these creatures are very fragile and can be harmed by you if you are not careful. Snorkelers are lucky to be able to see the underwater world up close. But because you are close, you must be especially careful not to disturb anything. We should all try to be **Eco-Champion snorkelers**. An "Eco-Champion" snorkeler is one who protects the underwater environment. It's easy and fun to become an "Eco-Champion" snorkeler. Here are the things that will make you an Eco-Champion Snorkeler:

1. Whenever you want to snorkel in a new area, ask someone in charge for an **orientation**. An orientation explains what water conditions and marine creatures may be found in the area, and what the rules are to protect those creatures.

2. Do not touch the coral in any way. This means not standing on, sitting on, handling, or kicking coral. Remember– it may take thousands of years for damaged coral to be replaced.

3. Do not remove coral, shells, or rocks for souvenirs. Remember that you may be taking away a creature's home!

4. Do not wear gloves. If your snorkeling guide says it's OK to pet the fish and marine mammals, such as dolphin, pet them very gently with your bare hand. The rough surface of a glove may rub off the fish's outer coating which it needs to protect itself from infection (fish can get sick just like people!).

5. Your snorkeling instructor will show you the right way to kick with your fins. It is important that you **DO NOT KICK** the coral. It is also important that your fins do not stir up a lot of sand. When sand is kicked up, it can float down and lay on the coral. When sand lays on the coral, it blocks out the sunlight which the coral needs to make its food. If coral becomes completely covered with sand, it may suffocate and die.

6. Fish are beautiful and fun to watch, but do not try to feed them. People food could make them sick.

7. Do not grab or ride on a sea turtle. Even though you only want to play, you may frighten the sea turtle or harm it.

Besides protecting the marine life when your are snorkeling, there are other important things an Eco-Champion can do. To learn more, turn to the back of the book.

By being an Eco-Champion snorkeler, everyone of us can help protect our planet's waters. You may think, **"the ocean is such a large place and I'm only one small person. Can I really make a difference?"** Yes! You certainly can!

There's a story about a child who loved the ocean. One day he saw that his favorite beach was full of starfish which had been washed ashore in a storm. The little boy knew that unless the starfish were returned to the water they would die. Even though there were thousands of starfish and he was only one small person, the boy knew he had to try his best. He started to pick up the starfish, one at a time, and tossed each one as far out into the sea as he could throw. A man came by who saw what the boy was doing and laughed at him. "You're just wasting your time, kid," said the man as he pointed to the thousands of lost starfish lying on the beach. "It won't matter." As the child picked up the next starfish he answered, "It matters to this one!"

Now that you are an "Eco-Champion" who will help keep our oceans safe and beautiful, let's learn how to snorkel and have fun in the water!

CHAPTER 2

The Stuff
We Need
for Snorkeling

Snorkeling EQUIPMENT

THE SNORKELER'S EQUIPMENT

THE STUFF WE NEED FOR SNORKELING

THE MASK

Why do we wear a mask when we snorkel? To **see**!! But, how does a mask help us see well underwater? How does a mask work?

When you open your eyes underwater you can't see well because human eyes aren't made to see through water like dolphin or fish eyes. But when you put on your face mask, you put an **air space** between your eyes and the water. This air space allows you to see through the air (like you do on land) and into the water. You can look into the water with your mask on just like you look into an aquarium, except you are in the water, the aquarium is all around you!

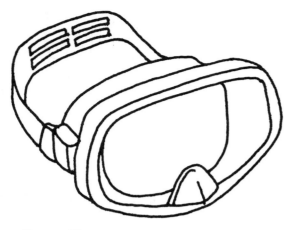

When choosing a mask, be sure it is a full face mask with an enclosed nose pocket. It should be made of soft rubber or silicon with "tempered" glass, a nice double strap, and sturdy buckles. The most important thing when choosing your mask is that the mask **fits**. You can tell if a mask fits by a simple mask fitting test called the **sniff test**.

THE SNIFF TEST

1. Hold the mask up to your face without the strap around your head.

2. Inhale gently through your nose and let go with your hands.

3. Does the mask stay on your face? If it does, it fits. If the mask falls off, it leaks air somewhere and does not fit. Be sure your hair is out from under the mask because your hair could cause an air leak even when the mask fits properly.

The Snorkel

Breathing is easy when you are on land. In fact, you hardly even think about it. Underwater, or even in the water, it is different. Lifting your mouth out of the water to breathe takes a lot of work which can tire you out. With a snorkel you can breathe with your **head down** and your eyes can look at the beautiful and interesting things in the water **without** getting too tired.

Using Your Snorkel

There are several parts of the snorkel that will make it easy for you to use. The mouthpiece should be very **comfortable** with a bite tab or a mouth ring which can be held easily between your teeth. The snorkel should be moveable so you can fit it into your mouth. It should have a gentle curve so breathing will be easy. A bright marking near the top will help you to be seen easier when you are in the water. The diameter of the snorkel, called the "bore," should be large enough to let enough air through and make breathing easy. If you are a small person, the bore should not be too large as this can make "clearing" difficult (more on this later). A snorkel keeper should be attached to the snorkel to hold it to the mask strap.

You may have played with fins in the pool. Fins make your feet look like a duck's feet and sure help you go **fast**! Fins work by making your feet bigger.

This helps you push through the water easier. There are many types of fins. The fins that are best for you are the ones that fit and are really comfortable.

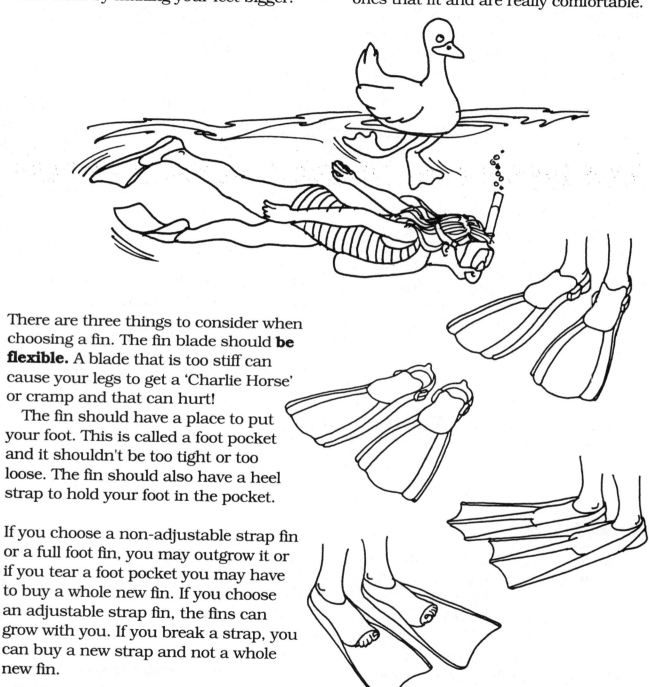

There are three things to consider when choosing a fin. The fin blade should **be flexible.** A blade that is too stiff can cause your legs to get a 'Charlie Horse' or cramp and that can hurt!

The fin should have a place to put your foot. This is called a foot pocket and it shouldn't be too tight or too loose. The fin should also have a heel strap to hold your foot in the pocket.

If you choose a non-adjustable strap fin or a full foot fin, you may outgrow it or if you tear a foot pocket you may have to buy a whole new fin. If you choose an adjustable strap fin, the fins can grow with you. If you break a strap, you can buy a new strap and not a whole new fin.

THE SNORKELING VEST

How would you like to own your own little island? Imagine every time you go snorkeling you can bring your own island with you. It is called a snorkeling vest. Snorkeling vests come in many shapes and sizes and the best vest for you is the one that fits you and is really comfortable.

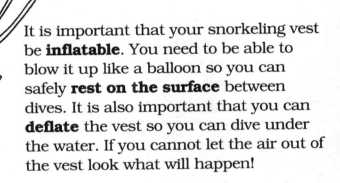

It is important that your snorkeling vest be **inflatable**. You need to be able to blow it up like a balloon so you can safely **rest on the surface** between dives. It is also important that you can **deflate** the vest so you can dive under the water. If you cannot let the air out of the vest look what will happen!

THINGS A GOOD SNORKEL VEST SHOULD HAVE

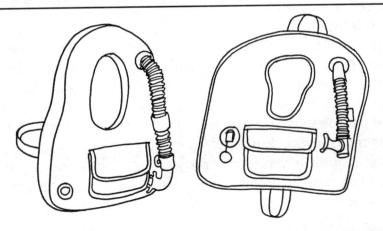

There are several things you should look for when choosing a snorkeling vest. The vest should have an **inflator hose** with a comfortable **mouthpiece**.

It should have a **waist strap** to keep it close to your body. Some vests have another strap called a **crotch strap** that will also help to keep the vest snug.

Chlorine water, salt water and sunshine are not very kind to snorkeling equipment. To help your gear last a long time in good condition you should follow these simple rules:

1. Always rinse your gear off with fresh water after using it in a chlorine pool or salt water. Make sure you rinse the inside of your snorkeling vest, too.

2. Dry your gear in a cool and shady area away from the sun and heat.

3. Store your gear neatly away from sun and heat.

A gear bag will keep your equipment in one place. This will make it easy for you to carry your gear to a dive site. Mark your equipment so you can find it if it gets lost or mixed up with your buddy's gear. Rubber paint or plastic tape make good markings.

REMEMBER! Choosing the right snorkeling equipment for yourself is very important. To have the most fun snorkeling and to be a safe snorkeler, your equipment must fit and be very comfortable. The best place to buy your snorkeling gear is at a professional dive shop. The people who work at the dive shop are experts and can assist you in choosing the right equipment.

The most important things to remember when choosing your snorkeling equipment is how it **fits**, how it **feels**, how it **works** for **you**, and how much you **like it!**

CHAPTER 3

SNORKELING

Skills

Learning to Snorkel is Easy!

THE BUDDY SYSTEM

Sharing experiences with a **buddy** is part of what makes snorkeling fun! The **buddy system** is one of the most important things a safe snorkeler learns in the pool and practices in openwater.

The **buddy system** is the number one rule of diving. **ALWAYS SNORKEL WITH A BUDDY**. Buddies are very useful. Checking equipment, answering questions, being close in case of trouble, and sharing experiences are all the jobs of a good diving buddy.

A **buddy check** is done before entering the water. Your buddy **checks** your mask and snorkel as well as your fins and snorkeling vest. If you are using a weight belt and wetsuit, your buddy checks them for you, too (we'll discuss this more later on). What does a buddy check? Your buddy makes sure all of your gear works properly and is adjusted to fit you. Your buddy also checks to see that you have put your gear on **correctly.** Your buddy needs to know how your gear works. You will then **check** the same things for your buddy. You and your buddy do this **before** you ever get into the water.

1. THE MASK AND SNORKEL

make sure the strap is secure and the snorkel is attached firmly with the snorkel keeper

2. THE FINS

make sure the straps are adjusted properly and that the straps are good and strong.

3. THE SNORKELING VEST

make sure the vest holds air and has no leaks. Check the straps and make sure they are snug and comfortable.

When in the water, each buddy takes a turn diving underwater. This is called the **ONE UP, ONE DOWN** method. Buddy #1 signals to Buddy #2 that they are making a dive. When the dive is done and Buddy #1 has returned to the surface, it is Buddy #2's turn. The buddy on the surface can keep an eye open for waves or boats or anything unusual that the buddy underwater can't see. Both buddies can take a break to share what they have seen underwater and to rest together. It takes some practice to stay together as buddies, but every dive is a fun practice session.

ENTRIES - GETTING INTO THE WATER

GIANT STRIDE

- from medium to high places
- if you do not know bottom
- if you know depth

BACK ROLL

- from low places
- from small boats
- if you know water depth and bottom

FRONT ROLL

- if you know bottom
- from low places
- if you know water depth

HEAD FIRST DIVE

- if you know the bottom
- if you know the depth
- efficient and quick dive

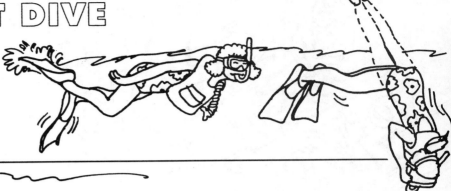

TUCK DIVE

- if you know the bottom
- if you know the depth
- if you do not want any splash

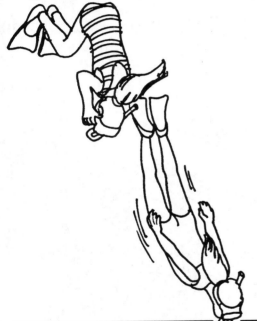

FEET FIRST DIVE

- when diving in kelp
- if you are unsure of bottom
- if you are unsure of depth

THE SNORKEL DIVE

If your mask is bumped while you are diving and fills with water, you can easily clear it. Sometimes it is easier to come to the surface and reseal the mask against your face, but it is fun to know how to clear your mask underwater. The steps are:

1. Reseal the mask against your face, making sure all hair and straps are out from underneath the mask.

2. Look down and press the top of the mask against your face, so the air you are about to put in the mask doesn't escape but water can escape from the bottom. This also keeps water from going up your nose!

3. Exhale or blow gently through your nose. This makes the water in the mask leave under the bottom of the mask. The air you put in will stay and the mask will fill with air.

4. Slowly tilt your head and mask towards the surface, as you exhale through your nose. This will remove the last bit of water. No water will be left inside your mask!

Mask clearing is a skill you can practice. Snorkelers like to be able to clear their masks underwater as well as on the surface. It's fun!

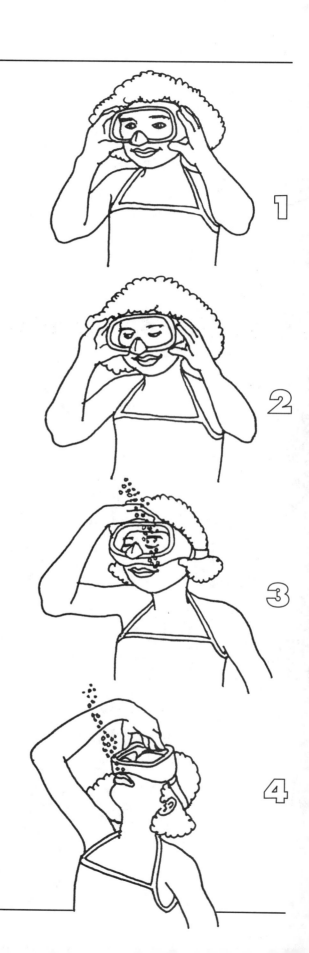

KICKING WITH FINS

Fins make your feet bigger and bigger feet can make you swim faster and dive deeper when you are snorkeling. Fins can also make you clumsy and cause you to get a leg cramp or Charlie Horse if you don't kick them correctly.

It will take some practice to get your leg muscles used to your new big feet, but soon you will be able to swim like a seal!

There are two types of kicks that snorkelers use:

THE MODIFIED FLUTTER KICK

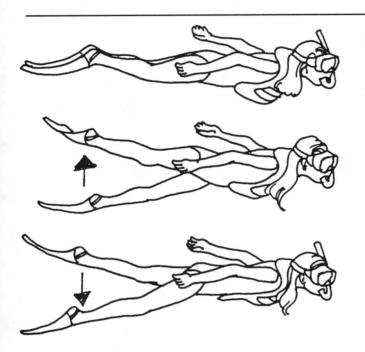

The **Modified Flutter Kick** is the easiest kick. This kick is like the one you do when you swim, only much **slower**. This is the magic of kicking with fins. The slower and **deeper** you kick the farther and faster you will go!

Move your legs up and down from the hips letting your strong thigh muscles move the bottom of your legs and fins. Keep your knees bent slightly and your arms at your side.

THE DOLPHIN KICK

The **Dolphin Kick** is used for moving quickly underwater. This kick uses your entire body and is a lot of Fun! Have you ever seen a snake as it slides across the ground? The snake's body moves back and forth **sideways**. We do the same thing only **up and down**.

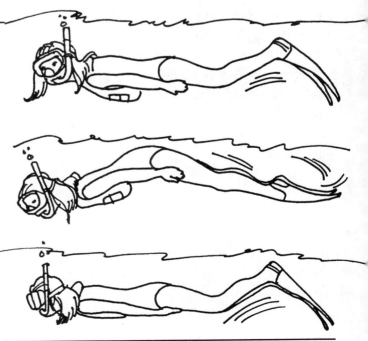

CLEARING YOUR SNORKEL

When you dive below the surface, your snorkel will fill with water. As you return to the surface you can **blow out** the water. When you blow out or **clear** the water from your snorkel you can breathe through it as soon as you reach the surface. There are two ways you can clear your snorkel when surfacing:

THE WHALE BLAST

When you reach the surface you toss your head forward and blow air through your snorkel in a big blast!

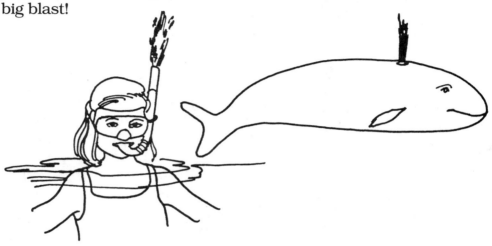

THE DOLPHIN PUFF

As you near the surface begin to gently exhale air into your snorkel. The air will push the water out of the bottom. When you reach the surface gently toss your head forward and puff. It's so easy, it's magic!

CHAPTER 4

PRESSURE

How We
Avoid the
Big Squeeze

PRESSURE
THE BIG SQUEEZE

As you dive below the surface, the water surrounds you and presses on your body. This pressure affects your body's **air spaces.** Air spaces are found in your **sinuses, lungs** and **ears.** Your air spaces are squeezed by this extra pressure. Don't worry! You will learn how to **equalize** the pressure so it won't squeeze. You can't feel the squeeze in your lungs or sinuses because they adjust themselves.

Your ears may feel like something is pressing on them. They will become **uncomfortable** if you don't equalize. You may have felt this when you dove to the bottom of a deep swimming pool. Some people can feel the pressure squeeze in their ears' **air space** more than others. Your ears feel different because the water surrounding you squeezes the air space in your ears. This causes your ear drums to stretch. Stretching the ear drum too much can hurt. Not good!

This is a picture of the ear **air space** and the **ear drum.** Notice that the normal ear does not have a stretched ear drum. The other ear has a very stretched ear drum. **OUCH!**

YOU CAN PREVENT EAR SQUEEZES. Simply **equalize** the pressure in the inside section of your ears' air space with the outside pressure.

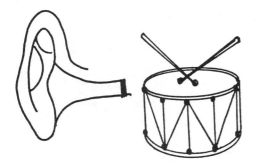

To **equalize** your ear air space: **close** the air exits in your nose and mouth by gently pinching your nose and closing your mouth. **Exhale gently** directing air into the middle ear air space. You will feel the change and you may hear a popping sound like when you go up in an elevator in a tall building. It is important to learn to exhale gently. After some practice, many snorkelers can equalize simply by swallowing.

Practice is the most important part. Start equalizing on every dive **before** you feel pressure in your ear. Continue to equalize until you are as deep as you want to be. Your ears should **never hurt.** If they do, you should come up, end the dive, and rest.

CHAPTER 5

HYPOTHERMIA

How We Keep from Getting Cold

HYPOTHERMIA

How We Keep From Getting Cold

HYPO = too little
THERMIA = body heat
HYPOTHERMIA = too little body heat

Hypothermia is the lowering of the body core temperature so much that the body cannot heat itself up again. When you get cold you begin to **shiver.**

Shivering is the way the body tries to warm itself. If your body gets too cold even the shivering will stop and hypothermia will occur. This can happen to snorkelers in warm water as well as cold water if they stay in too long.

The most dangerous thing about **Hypothermia** is that a person who has hypothermia may not know it. They may just seem grumpy, clumsy or confused. They may not even be shivering anymore because they may not even feel **cold** anymore.

You can Avoid Hypothermia by:

1. Getting out of the water when you or your buddy start to get too cold.
2. Wearing proper body protection such as a wetsuit.
3. Watching how your buddy is acting. Get out of the water if your buddy begins to shiver uncontrollably or act funny.

Here's what you can do if you think you or your buddy has **Hypothermia**:
1. **CALL FOR HELP**. Call a lifeguard, policeman or an adult for help right away.
2. Get out of your wet suit or swimming suit and **get dry**.
3. Put on warm dry clothes.
4. **Drink warm liquids**.

Signs of Hypothermia are:

1. Shivering - it is the body's first try to warm itself up.
2. Numbness - especially in fingers and toes.
3. Pain.
4. Weakness.
5. Confusion.
6. Unconsciousness.
7. **DEATH!**

> **REMEMBER:**
> **TO AVOID HYPOTHERMIA**
> **GET OUT OF THE WATER**
> **WHEN YOU BEGIN**
> **TO GET COLD**

CHAPTER 6

HYPERVENTILATION

Can We
Breathe
Too Much?

HYPERVENTILATION
CAN WE BREATHE TOO MUCH?

HYPER = too many or (too big)
VENTILATION = breaths or breathing
HYPERVENTILATION = too many breaths

Breathing is very important. We need to breathe **air**. Air is part **oxygen**. It is oxygen that keeps our hearts pumping and our brains thinking. When we **inhale** we are taking in oxygen as part of the air we breathe.

In our lungs the oxygen part of the air gets into our blood. Our blood acts **like a bus.** As the bus travels around our body, the oxygen gets off and helps the heart to pump, the body to move, the lungs to breathe, and the brain to think. As the oxygen gets off the bus, used oxygen or **carbon dioxide** gets on the bus and goes back to our lungs. When we **exhale** we are letting the used oxygen, which is now **carbon dioxide,** out of our body.

Your brain knows when to inhale and exhale by the amount of carbon dioxide it feels in your lungs. When you breathe your lungs are filled with fresh oxygen. As the oxygen is replaced by carbon dioxide, your brain tells you to take another breath.

When you exhale the carbon dioxide, you finish the breathing cycle. With every new breath, the body starts the cycle again. We call this cycle the **breathing cycle**. Since this happens every time we breathe, how can we take too many breaths? How can we **hyperventilate**?

If we **change** our normal **breathing cycle** we can hyperventilate. Our breathing cycle can change if we get excited or scared. It can change if we're exercising too hard. If we change our normal breathing cycle by taking more than 3 or 4 quick deep breathes in a row, we can hyperventilate.

Hyperventilating is a way of tricking the brain into thinking that the body does not need to breathe. If we hyperventilate, the carbon dioxide leaves our body too fast. Without enough carbon dioxide to tell the brain to breathe, the brain thinks the body does not need oxygen.

What could happen to a snorkeler after hyperventilation? Most likely, the snorkeler would not feel the need to breathe because their brain was tricked. The brain would stop thinking because it could not get the oxygen it needs.

When the brain stops thinking, the body cannot get any messages from the brain. The body stops and becomes **unconscious.** Unconscious means that the brain is not thinking and the body is not able to move.

Hyperventilating is **dangerous** for snorkelers. Imagine falling asleep while under the water! Not healthy. Snorkelers that do not know about hyperventilation can become unconscious in the water. This is called **shallow water blackout.** It can happen in shallow as well as deep water. Snorkelers **should not hyperventilate.**

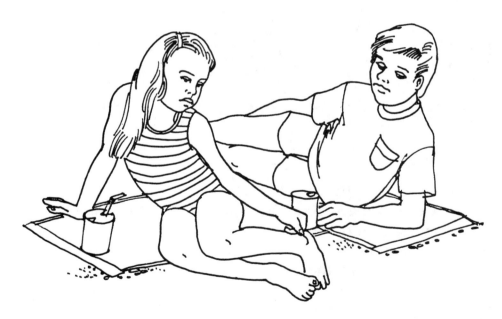

PREVENT SHALLOW WATER BLACKOUT BY FOLLOWING THESE FOUR SAFETY RULES

1. Do not hyperventilate. Always breathe normally.
2. End a dive when you feel the need to breathe.
3. Stay in good diving shape and practice snorkel diving often.
4. Rest and relax between dives.

How can we stay underwater longer if we shouldn't hyperventilate?

Snorkelers can stay underwater longer by strengthening their lungs and bodies with **practice.** The more we practice snorkeling, the longer our lungs and bodies will be able to work without breathing. Just as practicing helps us become stronger, practicing underwater swimming and **breath hold diving** will help our lungs become stronger. Our bodies get stronger a little bit at a time so we must remember to practice as often as we can. If we can't go snorkeling we should practice by swimming in a pool or doing other fun exercise.

Safe snorkelers prevent **shallow water blackout** by following the four safety rules when snorkeling. When practicing, remember the four **safety rules** and the four **safety hints** listed on the previous page. Strong, safe snorkelers practice on every dive whether in the pool or open water.

WHEN PRACTICING SNORKEL DIVING AND SWIMMING, IT IS IMPORTANT TO:

1. Always practice with a buddy.
2. Always have a life guard or instructor watching you. Tell someone what you are going to be doing.
3. Work up to longer dives by practicing shorter ones first.
4. Take plenty of rest time between each practice dive.

CHAPTER 7

OVEREXERTION

Too Much
Exercise
Isn't Good

OVEREXERTION

Too Much Exercise Isn't Good

OVER = too much
EXERTION = exercise
OVEREXERTION = too much exercise

Exercise is healthy. Our bodies and brains need exercise. Running, swimming, and playing sports are good exercises. **Snorkeling is very good exercise.** Exercise strengthens your body and keeps you feeling healthy. But too much exercise can be painful. Too much exercise at one time is called **overexertion.**

Everyone of us is **unique**. Everyone one of us is **special**. Everyone one of us has our own strengths and weaknesses. You know that sometimes you are able to snorkel and dive underwater longer than your buddy. Some buddies get tired very soon and others never seem to get tired at all. To prevent over exertion (exercising too much) you need to know the strengths and weaknesses of your buddy and yourself.

To Prevent Overexertion:

1. Snorkel within your abilities.
2. Practice often.
3. Stay in good health.
4. Get lots of rest before snorkeling.
5. Wear the proper equipment.

Snorkel Within Your Abilities

A snorkeler knows how well he or she can dive. No one knows more about **you** than **you**. The best judge of how long and hard you will be able to exercise is you. Decide how long you are able to stay in the water, decide how long you are able to stay down underwater, and **tell** your buddy. Your buddy will tell you his or her ability, and you will then be able to have a **SAFE** enjoyable snorkeling adventure. **Snorkel within your ability.**

Practice often and stay in good health. Practice is very important to help you to keep your snorkel diving skills as good as they can be. Practice also improves endurance and strengthens your body. Snorkelers should dive only when they are in good shape and feel healthy. If a snorkeler has a cold, is tired, or just does not feel good, they should not go diving. A snorkeler who has not gone diving in a while can practice and review snorkeling skills in a pool before going diving in open water.

It is important to be sure of your ability and skills and to know that you are able to perform them well.

1. **A Safe Snorkeler— dives within his or her abilities.**

2. **A Safe Snorkeler— practices often.**

3. **A Safe Snorkeler— does not dive when not feeling well.**

CHAPTER 8

Additional EQUIPMENT

Extra Stuff that
Makes Us Safer
Snorkelers

ADDITIONAL EQUIPMENT

EXTRA STUFF THAT MAKES US SAFER SNORKELERS

Masks, fins, snorkels and snorkeling vests are fine in warm, heated pools where a lifeguard is on duty. But when we seek snorkeling adventure in our local pond, lake, river or ocean we may need more equipment. For **fun** and **safety** in the open water, snorkelers use additional equipment including **Wetsuits and Weight Belts.**

HOW A WETSUIT KEEPS YOU WARM

Wetsuits come in all shapes and sizes, to keep your body **warm.** Rubber **booties, gloves,** and **hoods** can also be worn for extra warmth. A wetsuit **protects** your body by **trapping** body heat. Wetsuits are made of rubber. The **thicker** the rubber, the more **protection** it gives, and the **warmer** it keeps you.

When you snorkel, water gets trapped between the suit and your skin. The water may feel cold but soon your body heats up the trapped water and you feel warm.

If you wear a suit that is too **large,** it will not keep the warmed up water close to your skin. If you wear a suit that is too **small,** it will not let in enough water and you will feel cold and uncomfortable. A wetsuit that is too small will pinch your skin, too.

A PROPER FITTING WETSUIT IS VERY IMPORTANT.

Remember, a wetsuit must **fit, feel good** and **work** for you. Ask your snorkeling instructor or a dive store professional for assistance in choosing the wetsuit that is right for you.

We now have our mask, fins, snorkel, snorkeling vest and wetsuit and we're ready to go snorkeling! Right? **Not Always!**

Remember how we are all different and unique? Well, some snorkelers float very easily. They are **positively buoyant.** And some snorkelers don't float as well. They are **negatively buoyant.**

To prevent **overexertion** and to be able to dive under the water easily, snorkelers need to be **neutrally buoyant.** Neutral means that we do not float and we do not sink. We are in between floating and sinking. To find out if we are positive or negative, we can take a **buoyancy test**. It's very easy!

THE BUOYANCY TEST

1. Float vertical in the water with your snorkel in your mouth.
2. Take a big deep breath and hold it. (Your lungs will act like balloons and you should float high in the water.)
3. Now exhale all the air in your lungs.

If you still **float high**: you are **positive**. If you **sink below** the water: you are **negative**. If you **sink a little** (the water is at eye level): you are **neutral**.

You can use this Buoyancy Test to decide if you need to wear a weight belt. If you are **neutral** or **negative** you do not need a weight belt. If you are **negative**, you need to put some air into your snorkeling vest until you are neutral. If you are **positive** you need to wear a weight belt.

Most snorkelers need to wear a weight belt when using a wetsuit because the wetsuit rubber is filled with millions of little air bubbles which makes it **positive**. Since we cannot **deflate** our wetsuits like we do our snorkeling vests, we must add a **weight belt**.

A snorkeler wearing a wetsuit decides how much weight to wear by doing the buoyancy test and either **adding weight** or **taking weight off** until the belt is adjusted so that the snorkeler is **neutrally buoyant.**

Weight belts are usually made of colorful nylon webbing and come with a **quick release buckle.** The buckle allows you to drop the weight belt quickly if you should ever need to be **positively buoyant** fast.

The weight belt is designed to hold lead weights. Lead is very heavy and sinks. Most lead weights are grey, but some have colorful coating to make them easy to see. Weights come in several styles including curved **hip weights, square weights,** and **bullet weights**.

Weight **keepers** are used to **keep** the weights in position so they will be comfortable around your waist during the dive. Keepers also help keep the weights from sliding off the end of the belt when you are putting on the belt.

Safe snorkelers always:

1. Put the weight belt on **last**, after every other piece of equipment is in place and ready. Nothing should be put on **over** the belt.

2. Practice dropping the weight belt **before** every dive. Watch out for your toes! It is part of the **buddy check**.

3. Always **drop** the weight belt in any emergency. Always drop your buddy's belt if he or she is in need of help (we'll discuss this in the next chapter).

With your wetsuit and weight belt, you have two new things to check before entering the water to snorkel. Your **buddy check** now becomes even more important.

Let's review our **buddy check**:
1. Check the straps and buckles on the mask and fins. Make sure they are in good condition and adjusted to fit correctly.
2. Make sure the snorkel is attached firmly to the mask strap with a snorkel keeper.
3. Check for leaks in the snorkeling vest by inflating it and listening at the seams. Also check that the straps are adjusted to fit correctly.
4. Check the wetsuit for proper fit.
5. Check the weight belt to make sure the weights are on firmly and the buckle releases properly. Do a **quick draw** release.

Practice releasing the weight belt as quickly as possible. Do this for every **buddy check,** before every dive, and before each pool practice session.

When you and your buddy have completed the **buddy check** and are sure that all of the equipment works properly and is adjusted to fit well, you are ready to **snorkel!**

> **REMEMBER! CHECK YOUR BUDDY'S EQUIPMENT AND YOUR OWN EQUIPMENT BEFORE GETTING IN THE WATER.**

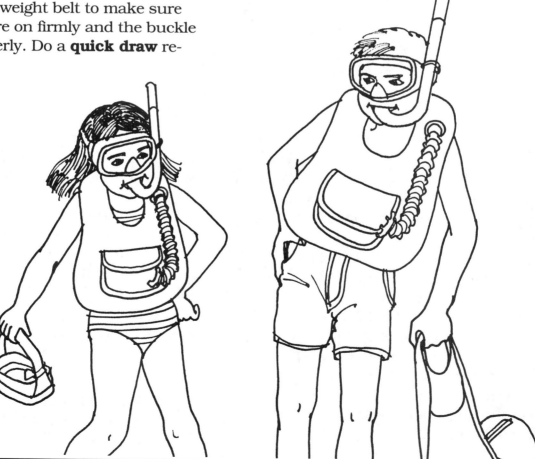

Snorkelers who plan to dive in open water areas such as lakes, ponds, rivers, and oceans should use some additional safety equipment. A **surface float** is one of the most important pieces of safety equipment that can be taken when on a snorkeling adventure.

Surface floats are small islands that can be towed or pushed along to your dive site. They provide a place to **rest** between dives. The float can be tied to an anchor or buoy or left to float along with the snorkeler in calm water. When used with a **dive flag**, the float warns boaters and skiers that you are snorkeling in the area and that they should stay away.

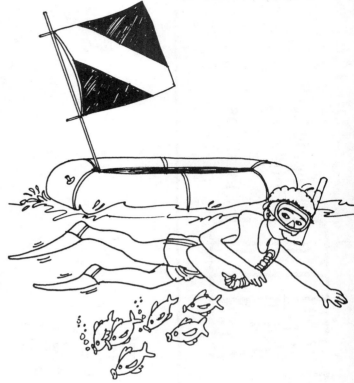

The **diver's flag** is red with a white stripe from the upper left corner to the lower right corner. The flag should stand high above the float so that boaters can see it.

A buddy team should have at least one surface float with dive flag between them. Surface floats are used for the safety of snorkelers.

Surf mats, innertubes, boogie boards, surfboards, and **small inflatable boats** make good surface floats.

Anything that floats well and can be towed easily out to the dive site will make a proper surface float.

A SURFACE FLOAT WITH DIVE FLAG SHOULD BE USED BY SNORKELERS ON EVERY OPEN WATER DIVE

CHAPTER 9

Snorkeling FIRST AID

Helping Your Buddy Out of Sticky Situations

RED CROSS
CPR
CLASS
TODAY 1:00PM
AUDITORIUM

I ♥ TO SNORKEL

FIRST AID

LEARN CPR

SNORKELING FIRST AID

HELPING YOUR BUDDY OUT OF STICKY SITUATIONS

Sometimes snorkelers can get into sticky situations and need help. Feeling tired, seasick, or getting a cramp or Charlie Horse in open water may surprise even a well-prepared snorkeler. These are the times when a good buddy is really nice to have around. If you get into such a situation, your buddy can help you by finding out what the problem is and helping solve the problem safely.

When your buddy shows signs of distress, you need to help right away. **Ask** your buddy "**ARE YOU OK?**" or "**CAN I HELP YOU?**" Talking to your buddy in a **quiet voice** can calm them if they begin to get panicky. **Panicky** means they are very nervous and not acting as they normally would.

There are several situations that can cause your buddy to get panicky:

1. Snorkeler is wearing **too much weight** and is finding it hard to keep on the surface.

2. Snorkeler has a **leg cramp** or Charlie Horse.

3. Snorkeler **swallows water** and begins to cough.

4. Snorkeler gets **tired** or starts to get **seasick**.

If your buddy is too heavy, **inflate** their snorkeling vest. If they still have problems staying on the surface, **drop** their weight belt. If your buddy has a leg cramp, **massage** and stretch the cramped muscle and safely assist them to shore or boat. If your buddy begins to cough from swallowing water, inflate their snorkeling vest and rest on the surface until everything is OK again.

If your buddy is tired, seasick, or just not feeling right, you can **reassure** and **calm** them while towing them to safety. There are two types of tows to use when towing a snorkeler to safety.

THE ARMPIT CARRY

This carry is done by grabbing the armpit of the tired buddy with your hand, thumb up, and pushing towards shore, boat or other safe place. Be careful to use your right hand with the buddy's right armpit, or left hand to left armpit. This way the buddy may lay back in the water and relax and you can maintain eye contact and talk with your buddy.

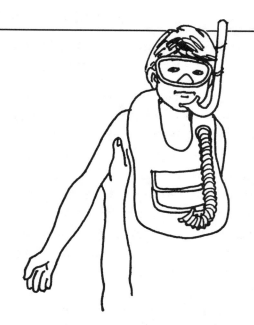

THE WHEELBARROW PUSH

This carry is like pushing a wheelbarrow. By putting the snorkeler's fins under your armpits and holding the lower part of the legs you can easily push them towards safety while they lay back in the water. Having a full snorkeling vest and arching the back will help the tired snorkeler be more comfortable.

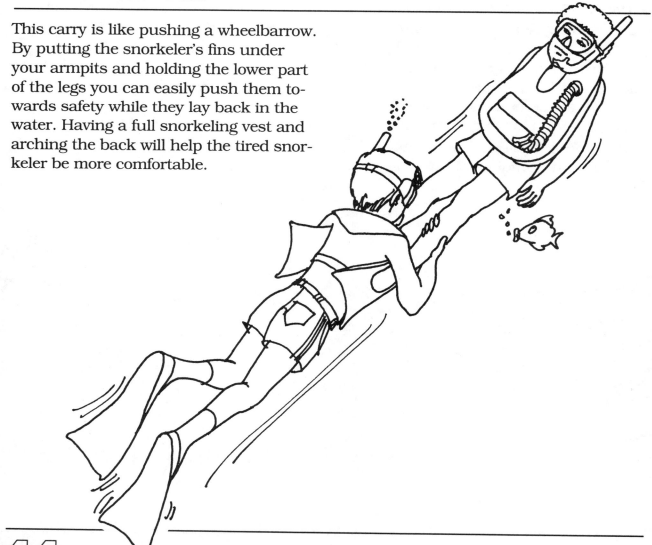

When doing each of these carries, remember your buddy is in need of reassurance. Keep good **eye contact** and **talk** to your buddy. Tell them about where and how close safety is. This will help them to feel much better.

The Armpit Carry and Wheelbarrow Push are done when a tired snorkeler needs aid and is still conscious and breathing.

A diver who does not answer when you ask "**ARE YOU OK?**" and appears to be sleeping in the water may be in serious trouble. Quickly drop their weight belt, inflate the snorkeling vest and remove their snorkel and mask. Immediately start yelling for **HELP!** Wave your arms to get someone's attention on the shore or pool deck. After you are sure help is on the way start towing your buddy to shore.

A Smart Snorkeler is Always Prepared

We recommend that snorkelers take a first aid course at their local American Red Cross or YMCA. It could be very important to your buddy someday for you to learn how to do Mouth to Mouth Resuscitation and CPR. Also learn how to care for simple injuries like scrapes from coral and sunburn. This will make you a really **great buddy!**

CHAPTER 10

Planning A SNORKELING Adventure

Where To Go and What To Do

PLANNING A SNORKELING ADVENTURE

WHERE TO GO AND WHAT TO DO

DIVE = underwater fun!
PLANNING = organizing for safety
DIVE PLANNING is done for fun, safe, organized diving!

Snorkelers want to dive safely and have a lot of fun every time they go snorkeling. It is important to **plan** each snorkeling adventure. **Safety** is the most important point to think about when planning a diving day. When snorkelers plan their dives and dive their plans they have more fun and avoid unsafe diving.

The three areas of your diving day to plan are **before the dive, at the dive site and after the dive.**

Before you really **go** snorkeling, you and your buddy should have a dive plan.

Most important is to check your equipment to make sure every piece of gear works properly. Organize your gear in one area or in your gear bag. This will help you to remember everything. It would not be fun if you got to the dive site and had no mask. If you need to rent or borrow any additional equipment, arrange for it now. It is polite to ask for or reserve any rented or borrowed equipment to be sure it will be available for the dive.

After the equipment is checked and arranged, be sure your buddy has done the same thing. When your buddy is ready, you will need to make a few decisions: Where to go, what to bring, how long to stay, and what to do if the weather is poor. You can even call the lo-cal dive shop for a report on the diving conditions.

The shop will know where the diving is best and the most recent conditions.

This information will help you plan. It will also help you decide to dive another day if the diving weather is poor.

It is important that you get permission to go on your snorkeling adventure from someone responsible. They can also help you plan your adventure. Having someone else concerned about your safety is a nice feeling. We'll call this person our **dry buddy**.

Once at the dive site, the first thing snorkelers must do is to check the water conditions. Do not put on your gear only to find it is too rough to dive. Get to a high viewpoint where you can see the entry and exits points as well as the entire diving area. Observe the size of the waves, any rip currents, and water visibility. Note any boats or other hazards. You should **know** the dive site. At this point, **decide to go, or not to go**.

If the waves are too big or the water too murky for you and your buddy to snorkel comfortably and safely, **DON'T GO SNORKELING!** Remember that you must snorkel within your abilities. If you decide not to go diving, then you can do whatever else was planned. This might include bodysurfing (if it is safe enough), exploring the beach area, playing games (such as frisbee and football), and having a fun day. If there is another dive site nearby which might be better, go and look at it. Otherwise, plan another diving day.

If you decide to go diving, gear up and do proper buddy checks. Watch the water action to see if conditions have changed at all since you last looked. Enter the water at the decided entry point and have a fun, safe dive. Always be aware of the changes which might happen since you got into the water. Watch your buddy and share your experiences with your buddy. It will then be **twice** as **fun**. When you are both ready to stop diving, exit at the decided or alternate exit spot.

Carefully take off your snorkeling gear and put it away. If fresh water is near, rinse the gear and pack it neatly in your gear bag. Now is the time to **share** your recent adventure with your buddy by recording your dive in your **logbook**.

Snorkelers and SCUBA divers keep logbooks as a permanent reminder of their diving activity. Logbooks are great for **show and tell**. Logbook information should include: dive site, dive buddy, date, weather and water conditions, and time spent in the water. Most important is what you saw under the water and the fun you and your buddy had snorkeling!

Your logbooks are very valuable proof of your adventures. They may become some of your most prized possessions and the only way you can truly share your dives with your non-diving friends. Take care of them!

Finally, after the dive is logged and the equipment is safe and neat, buddies can enjoy the rest of the day. Be sure to let your **dry buddy** know that you are finished snorkeling and are OK. Remember to thank your buddy and anyone who helped you by loaning equipment or providing rides to the site and back. You have returned from a dive safe and healthy and had **fun**! The dive plan worked and you are now ready to **plan another diving day!**

A safe snorkeler will always be prepared for any situation. The following items are good to have in your gear bag in case of a minor injury. Keep the items in a waterproof container or zip-lock bag to protect them.

- ☐ **Quarters for emergency phone calls**
- ☐ **List of emergency phone numbers**
- ☐ **Your home address and phone number**
- ☐ **Bandages (lots!)**
- ☐ **Sterile pads**
- ☐ **First aid tape**
- ☐ **Safety pins and needles**
- ☐ **Triangular bandage**
- ☐ **Soap**
- ☐ **First aid spray**
- ☐ **Safety Scissors**
- ☐ **Tweezers**
- ☐ **Medicated stick for lips**
- ☐ **Alcohol with glycerin (or anti-infection for ears)**
- ☐ **Sunscreen**

SPECIAL ITEMS

- ☐ **Vinegar Packets (for marine animal stings)**
- ☐ **Cleaning liquid (such as peroxide)**
- ☐ **Gauze scrub pads (medicated)**
- ☐ **First aid book**

DIVE PLAN CHECKLIST

BEFORE THE DIVE

- Get permission to go snorkeling
- Get equipment organized
- Check equipment to be sure it works properly
- Arrange for additional gear if needed
- Check with buddy and call local dive shop
- Decide where to go
- Decide what to bring
- Decide how long to stay
- Decide what to do if the weather is poor
- Arrange for transportation

AT THE DIVE SITE

- Check the diving conditions from a high viewpoint
- Decide on entry and exit points
- Choose an alternate exit point
- Observe waves, surf, wind, water visibility, weather

DECIDE TO DIVE OR NOT TO DIVE

If the decision is **not to dive:**
- Do the alternate activity planned
- Check the alternate dive site (if there is one)
- Plan another diving day

If the decision is **to dive:**
- Gear up and do proper buddy checks
- Enter water and **snorkel**
- Be aware of changing conditions and buddy
- Exit at decided exit point or alternate if necessary

AFTER THE DIVE

- Take off gear, rinse or put away to rinse at home
- Log the dive in the logbook and notify your dry buddy
- Thank everyone who helped including your **Buddy**

Plan Another Diving Day!

ECO-CHAMPION SNORKELERS CAN DO A LOT TO HELP MOTHER EARTH

In addition to protecting the marine life when you are in the water, there are other important things an Eco-Champion can do. You should practice these activities and share them with your family and friends. An Eco-Champion should always set a good example. These activities include:

1. Never throw garbage in the ocean, especially plastic. Plastic is not "biodegradable," which means that nature has a very hard time getting rid of it. Plastic can remain in the ocean for hundreds of years. Plastic bags, cups, balloons, six-pack holders, fishing line made of plastic, and other plastic items choke, entangle and kill fish, marine mammals and sea birds. Always make sure garbage is put in a trash receptacle and make it a point to cut up six-pack holders before you throw them out.

2. Take part in a beach cleanup. Cleanups are held at beaches, and also lakes and other bodies of water. Cleanups are helpful and fun activities for people of all ages, and they help remove things that are harmful to the environment. Ask your school or community center to organize a cleanup in your area. You can get free information on how to organize a cleanup from:

The Center for Marine Conservation
1725 DeSales Street NW
Washington, DC 20036

3. Collect books, newspaper stories, and magazine articles which talk about protecting the underwater world. Share this information with as many people as you can.

4. Make an album or portfolio of pictures which show the beauty and variety of the underwater world. After you learn to snorkel, you may learn to use an underwater camera, and create your own picture books. You may even become a famous underwater photographer someday!

5. Start an Eco-Champion club in your school or community center. The club can invite guest speakers who are experts in marine sciences.

6. Contact:
The Friends of the Coral Reef Club at:
The Center for Marine
Conservation, (CMC)
1725 DeSales Street, NW
Washington, DC 20036

CMC will send you a free fact sheet about coral, coloring pages and instructions on how to write a letter to Washington to encourage the government to protect coral reefs. If you send CMC a copy of your letter to the government, they will award you a colorful sticker and a "Friend of the Coral Reefs" certificate.

NOTES:

NOTES: